Blended Family Bliss

The Practical Guide to Blending Your Family

By
Ben R. Matthews, Esq.
with
David A. Kahn, MS, LPC, LPCS

PublishAmerica
Baltimore

© 2005 by Ben R. Matthews and David A. Kahn.
All rights reserved. No part of this book may be reproduced, stored in a retrieval system or transmitted in any form or by any means without the prior written permission of the publishers, except by a reviewer who may quote brief passages in a review to be printed in a newspaper, magazine or journal.

First printing

At the specific preference of the author, PublishAmerica allowed this work to remain exactly as the author intended, verbatim, without editorial input.

ISBN: 1-4137-9215-4
PUBLISHED BY PUBLISHAMERICA, LLLP
www.publishamerica.com
Baltimore

Printed in the United States of America

Dedication

This book is dedicated to the love of my life, my wife, Dotti. Not only was this book her idea, she is the true source for most of the advice you will find here and then we lived it out. I just wrote it down. And to Emily, Dorothy, Sean, Chris and Morgan, our children and blended family, they are a constant source of joy and inspiration.

Ben

My dedication goes to my wife, who placed her time and energy into helping to make final revisions and edits of this book and has always been my source of inspiration. I also dedicate this book to my children, David Jr., Celly Marshall, and Padgett who make me proud!

David

Acknowledgments

This book would not be in print without the guidance and gentle criticism of Philip Gardner. He saw some merit in a disorganized tangle of notes and showed me how to present them in a useful form.

And a special thanks to Ron and Gaby Harrelson, Lee and Robin Freeman, and Tim and Ann Norwood, blended families and dear friends, for their insight and encouragement.

Table of Contents

Blended Family Bliss

Introduction

Yes, you can find bliss in a blended family. You can even experience joy in being a stepparent. You are reading this page because you are, or someone you love is, about to begin raising a blended family. Perhaps you've already established your blended family and would like some extra guidance. You have some questions, concerns and maybe a few worries. Here's help.

Raising a traditional family is a challenge. Add to that the wonder of new love; mix in one or two measures of children, an assortment of relatives and an ex-spouse or two just to add spice and the fun has just begun. Blending a family is more challenging than raising a traditional family because of the large number, and the variety of, relationships each member of the family must deal with on a regular basis. In a traditional family you are a partner or spouse and you are a parent. There are probably two sets of grandparents including your parents and your in-laws. Your children may have brothers and/or sisters, parents and grandparents. Now let's look at your blended family. First of all you fill the same roles that you would in a traditional family. But there's so much more! Now you're also a step-parent, an ex-partner/spouse, an ex in-law and perhaps a co-parent — maybe twice! Your children may have a step-parent or two, one or two sets of step-brothers and sisters, and a number of new grandparents. There may even eventually be half brothers and sisters. Your children also have two homes, two bedrooms and two sets of rules.

How in the world do you and your partner create a family from this jumble of people? The answer is that you have to love and know your children. And you absolutely must give them time. Becoming a family will not happen overnight. Building relationships takes time and energy. And don't rule out seeking outside help from an expert. You would be amazed at the positive impact a therapist or counselor can have on the growth of your family. A few sessions may be just what you need to help your new family through the toughest times.

When my wife and I (I is usually Ben throughout the book) began our blended family a few years ago, we had trouble finding any helpful expert advice that was practical or positive. In fact, we joked that we would have to write the book ourselves. And here we are!

As you've probably already found out, there are plenty of people out there with opinions. But those opinions are not always helpful. The most helpful advice is practical advice. It offers skills and techniques you can actually implement. Helpful advice also needs to be presented in small doses. Like a beautiful rose, your family's flower will begin small. Gradually it will sprout new growth. Finally, after plenty of fertilizing and pruning, it will bud and bloom. Opinions and advice are like fertilizer. Too much and too soon will only result in burning the plant's delicate leaves.

In the following three sections of this book you will learn what we learned through on-the-job-training as the adult leaders in our blended family. Each section is devoted to one of the three major relationships within the blended family. First is your relationship as a couple—it is the most important relationship in the family. Secondly we'll address your relationship with the children, and last, your relationship with the other parents. Each section consists of thirteen or more topics designed to be easily digested and practical enough to be easily replicated.

The first section concerns your relationship with your partner, the primary relationship in the blended family. Without a strong relationship between you and your partner, your blended family will suffer. After all, it is the foundation for the family. Without a strong foundation the family is destined to suffer and crumble. In this section you will find some simple practical ideas to help build and maintain this precious relationship.

Section two is about raising the children. You will learn to take your children and your partner's children and blend all of them into a family. You'll also gain ideas that will help you create the feeling of family among the mix of people you have brought together. Some of the ideas you can apply to your family directly. Others may require that you adapt a little. But most of them will work for you if you persevere and use a little imagination.

The final section concerns your relationship with your children's other set of parents. Whether or not these people are reasonable, you must maintain some kind of working relationship with them. Here again you will find suggestions that will work for you. The focus is on living day-to-day with these people who have a place in your children's lives and, therefore, an impact on yours. It is always important to remember that even though you may no longer love or care for your ex, your children do and always will.

Remember what it was like having your first child. Amid all the excitement and hope you harbored fear and worry. Life got to be a bit of a blur those first couple of years. There were sleepless nights and times that you thought you'd never been so tired. There were tears, but there were smiles of joy and much laughter. Raising a blended family is a lot like that. It's just that there are a lot more people involved.

Section One
Build a Strong Relationship with Your Partner

In order to create a blissful blended family, you must build a strong relationship with your partner. Some are going to argue that you should focus on the children first, but the very best thing you can do for your children and your new children is to love your new partner.

A strong relationship is a relationship in which both partners know that the other loves them. They know because it is obvious from their partner's words and actions. Your actions demonstrate that you respect and care for your partner.

Isn't this why we began a new relationship in the first place? We have found someone to share our lives with both now and in the future. Good news. Choosing to raise a blended family can make your relationship stronger simply because of the skills you will master in building your family. You will have to work as a team, be considerate to one another, respect each other and above all communicate, communicate, communicate. These are skills that to one degree or another probably failed us in our previous relationships. David says that, "Many second marriages begin having trouble because one or both partners have not learned from the mistakes they made in their previous relationship." We have to stay aware that relationships are a constant work in progress. Communication is the key to identifying problems and creating solutions. Teamwork is non existent if only one member of the team feels there is a problem and tries to solve it on their own.

Your Children Benefit from a Strong Parental Relationship

When there is a strong, loving relationship between the parents in a blended family, their children develop a sense of stability. They are allowed to have this comfort because there is a low level of stress in the home. Adults in strong relationships address stressors in ways that protect their children. This protection frees the young people from feeling the full impact of anything that stresses the central relationship of the family, the core marriage. That allows us, the married couple, freedom to resolve conflict without dragging the children into it. And the fact that we discuss everything frees us to be honest with the children about certain situations because we have already discussed them together. Our familiarity lets us present a united front and gives our children confidence that, no matter what, they are taken care of.

Our children come out of households that were full of marital tension. Then they suffered the tension that came during the transfer from one house to another. And there may still be some anger between you and your ex. When you and your current partner talk every day, when you touch one another, and when you are considerate and respectful you create a home that is stable for the children because it is less stressful than the one they left. Your home is comfortable.

Loving your new children's parent will lead them to trust you. Let them see you love their mother. Let them see you love their father. Sharing and caring builds trust. The strong, healthy relationship you are building is the cornerstone of the new relationship you will have with your stepchildren. They will watch what you *do* before they commit to you or to their blended family. They know from experience that all marriages don't work out. Your actions will determine whether they open up to you or, instead, become defensive. When the children see the love in your actions, they will develop a trust for you and your marriage and they will commit to the blended family.

When you build a strong relationship with your partner, there is another more long-term benefit. Your relationship becomes a better model of adult relationships for the children. Your children are products of a failed relationship. And each of us had some responsibility for that relationship's failure. Unless you provide your children with a model of a good solid relationship, they may not see how it is done. Keep this is mind as you live with your partner. Ask yourself, "What actions do I want my children to imitate?" "What do I want to teach them about a loving, successful marriage?" With these thoughts in mind, I still open doors for my wife. I do it because I show her and our children that I respect and love her. From time to time my stepsons have copied this behavior. I hope that later on, they will open doors for their dates, girlfriends, and wives. We all know that children are great mimics. When we do the things that build a strong relationship, our children will respond to a good model for their adult lives.

We Benefit from a Strong Relationship

While building a strong relationship with your partner has great benefits for your children, it is you, the married couple, who primarily will benefit. Most of us hope to have a "'til death do us part" marriage with our soul mates. We don't stand at the altar planning to separate and divorce later in life. But experience has taught us that marriage doesn't always turn out like the fairytales do. *"And they lived happily ever after"* doesn't always apply. Our marriage won't mature gracefully *unless we constantly care for it.*

Love is not a feeling. Love is not an emotion. What love *is* is an action verb. By its very definition, love requires that something be *done*. We show love when we care for our partner. We care for our partner by sharing thoughts and feelings, showing respect, and being willing to work together. Sharing, showing respect, and working together will build a solid, adaptable relationship that can adjust to new situations. Your strong marriage will stand up against changes and crises of all kinds. You may even find that your marriage thrives when times are tough because you've become so accustomed to forming an alliance against whatever demands life makes.

We, as a couple, need the same sense of stability from the marital relationship that our children do. Perhaps you can recall from a previous relationship how it felt to return to a house at the end of the workday to be warmly greeted by the children and no one else. Maybe you preferred the days when one of you had to work late. These were stressful times. How wonderful it is to want to leave work early so you can get to your peaceful home and get a warm loving greeting from the children *and* your spouse. Building a strong relationship will not eliminate all stress, but it will help you deal with it in a constructive manner. As your relationship together grows and as you parent your children together, the stability you create will allow you to make a home where you and your children will find peace and comfort.

Love your partner by building a strong relationship. Love your children by building that strong relationship. Your children will see your love in your words and actions and will develop a sense of comfort and trust that will allow them to commit to the blended family and to you as a step-parent. You will benefit by creating a relationship that will last long after the kids are gone.

Talk Every Day

We all know successful relationships are built on good communication. When you examine your previous failed marriages it is very likely you will find some failure to honestly express yourself, or fully listen, or both. Marriages don't tend to fall apart overnight. It is usually the result of a consistent breakdown in communication or the failure to establish good communication habits.

Communication is a complex process and many couples blame their problems on the lack of communication. But if we watch them, they seem to have to no problems talking. In fact, they may be talking too much! Their problem isn't lack of communication. It's *interpretation*. People are like radios. We all have several antennae and receivers. Most of us think that communication only involves speaking and listening and, while these two components are important, they only make up 3% to 5% of all exchanges. The other 95% is non-verbal. That is why it is imperative that couples learn their partner's communication style. Couples may think they understand each other's words, but they mis-communicate because they mis-*interpret* the meaning and feelings behind the words. It is absolutely imperative that we take time to fully understand the message our partner is trying to convey before responding to it. It's so easy to jump to conclusions and assume we understand. If we are really honest with ourselves, we have to admit that sometimes it just feels good to think the other person is wrong. It's a selfish action not to be sure we understand before letting out an angry outburst. It's a selfish action to let our feelings be hurt just because we assume we know what the other person meant by his remark. Selfishness is an action. But so is love! Remember? Love is an action verb. To love, we have to *do* something. In order to do anything we have to *decide* to do it. We have to *determine* to do it. We must *choose* it. Take a moment and ask your partner what he or she meant. Find out if what you thought is true really is the truth. Just that one little act shows respect and thoughtfulness and, maybe you'll be pleasantly surprised by the answer you get.

It's so much nicer to talk through a disagreement by determining what your partner really means. An incorrect assumption based on unclear information creates a recipe for conflict that is not always easily settled. But by learning how to communicate effectively you will help all your relationships prosper. And in demonstrating your new communication skills in your marriage, you will model the behavior for all the children. They, in turn, will carry what they've learned into their adult relationships and a new, healthy cycle will have begun. Your choices today can affect the health of generations of marriages in your family!

The most effective tool in positive communication is the use of the Magic Statement. The magic statement focuses on what the person communicating feels, thinks, and wants rather than focusing on the person being communicated to. The statement simply goes:

"When this (situation) happens, I feel/think (fill in feeling or thought), because (fill in reason), and what I would like is (fill in specific behavior change)."

For example:

"When the garbage is not taken out, I feel like I am expected to do all the cleaning and that nobody cares about having a clean home except me. I need some help so I don't feel like I'm the only one working to have a nice home."

Notice that the word *you* is left out of the magic statement.

That is the most magic element of the statement. Not once in that statement was any particular person accused. No fingers were pointed. No blame was assigned.

Instead, it's all about *me*! *"I feel..." "I'm expected..." "I need..."*

This is one time when you have permission to talk about yourself. There is absolutely no cause for anyone to react to that statement defensively.

Let's try another one.

"When money is spent on big ticket items without us talking about it, I think our previous conversations about money have not been effective. What I would like is to come up with a way we can plan ahead for those big ticket items."

Remember this statement is a magic one, not a perfect one. If you apply this formula often and repeatedly you will notice a decrease in defensiveness on the part of anyone from whom you request behavior changes and you increase the chance that your message will not be misinterpreted or misunderstood.

None of us blend a family with the intention of tearing it apart later. It was bad enough the last time. So we simply must establish effective communication habits. It sounds so easy, doesn't it? Communication is simply the transfer of information. The key for your relationship to grow is the depth of information you share. Another way to look at it would be to gauge how personal the information you share is. You probably would not have committed to your partner unless you had each shared some hopes and dreams. Most of your conversations will not be deep and personal, but you need to place this type of communication as a regular priority in your lives to foster continued growth as a couple.

When Dotti and I were discussing getting married, we found that both of us believed we needed to improve our communication skills. So we promised each other to talk every day. Then we defined talking as discovering what went on in each other's day. We agreed not to accept easy answers like "It was fine." We promised to learn the details of the day and to express our thoughts and emotions about them. We agreed to hold each other to this promise. We have kept our promise. Over the years, as we have talked and shared, we have learned more about each other. We have dealt with issues as they arose. Our trust for each other has deepened and we have become each other's best friend.

Here's what you can do. Set a time to talk every day. You can choose a time by the clock or by your schedule. Don't be afraid to change the time. Early in our blended family life, we found that the best time for us was after the kids were in bed. Lately, because of a change in schedules, we talk right after the kids have left for school. You want a time when you are less likely to be interrupted so that you can pay attention to your partner. It is very difficult to pay attention to your partner if you are doing anything else. Don't set a minimum or a maximum amount of time for this.

This is a great time to plan. Talk about goals for your home. Perhaps there is a room that needs to be painted or a repair that needs to be made. Talk about your personal goals. Maybe one of you wants to work out everyday. Your partner can't support you in this goal if he doesn't know about it! Do you have goals for savings or retirement? Make vacation plans. Plan one with and one without kids! During this time you learn more about each other as you make serious plans and as you dream.

You will find that one of the benefits that comes from these talks with your partner is the support you'll get at unexpected times. My wife understands what it is like to deal with a difficult ex and, because she knows what I'm going through, I can handle those times better when I talk them over with her. The same holds true as we raise the children. Your partner's insights into what is happening with your children are often better than yours because he or she has a slightly different perspective, which helps. I've even been pleasantly surprised at how helpful Dotti has been when I experience problems at work. Even though she and I have very different careers, there have been times when we've been able to give each other insight into situations at work that we didn't think the other would have known anything about. Sometimes the advice comes through specific ideas, and sometimes we help each other just by listening. Having a sounding board when we need to vent or think out loud can be a very therapeutic thing! Try it. Ask your partner's permission to give and receive advice and then offer it as needed.

Another reason to talk every day is so you'll both know what is happening around your house. This is the day-to-day stuff, like who has a meeting or is taking someone to ball practice, music lessons, or theatre rehearsal. It can be important for each of you to know where the other is should something change. And, if your blended family is like mine, things can change quite rapidly! Rain can cancel practice or one of you may be asked to work later. Without regular and frequent communication, problems will arise!

You are used to sharing this kind of scheduling information. You can confirm which of you is doing what while getting ready for the day or you may find it easier to compare schedules the night before. Post a weekly schedule on the refrigerator or some other visible spot. List all of the appointments and activities for the day or the week. An online calendar like the one at www.familiez.com works really well, too. This helps avoid confusion and forgetfulness. Let your partner know of changes as they occur.

When you talk every day, your life will be smoother and your relationship with your partner will grow. Remember, it's the every day stuff that fertilizes your marriage. A seed doesn't bloom as soon as it's planted just as a marriage doesn't bloom on the wedding day. It takes daily sun, soil, and rain for a seedling to sprout, grow ever so slowly, and finally to bud and bloom. The plant will be even stronger if a good gardener pulls the weeds from around its roots. Marriages, like flowers, need the sunshine of warm smiles, the nourishing soil of communication and *interpretation,* and they definitely need to have their weeds pulled out every now and then, But if you are a faithful gardener, your marriage will bloom as beautifully as the most magnificent rose.

An important weed to pull from your marriage is pride. Please, don't be too proud to ask for help. It is so important to ask for help from your partner when you need it. Don't let yourself become overwhelmed because you won't admit when you've reached your limit. The thought behind this is: "I should be able to handle all of the responsibilities I have agreed to - all of the time!" or "It isn't fair for me to ask my partner to do something I am responsible for." Your unwillingness to ask for help actually denies your partner the chance to give to you through acts of service. By refusing to ask for help, you are denying him or her the *right* to be helpful. You are taking away an opportunity for your partner to *show love! You are actually selfishly withholding an opportunity from your spouse that could help you both grow!* Asking for help doesn't guarantee that your partner will be able to provide it, but it does give him- or her- the chance to try. Unless you ask for help, your partner may never know you needed it.

Pray Together

Your daily conversations will bring you and your partner closer. When you talk every day, you should also pray together. Not only is this an important part of your communication with the Lord, it is also indirect communication with your partner. The way you make yourself vulnerable in prayer with your partner will bind you to one another more strongly that you ever imagined. Just think! Being vulnerable makes you strong! The time you spend in prayer together becomes the most powerful relationship glue in the universe It's a marriage insurance policy you can't afford to ignore.

Maybe you and your partner aren't very religious. Maybe you think you'll feel silly. Or maybe one of you believes and the other one doesn't. That doesn't matter. Prayer is a different kind of communication. It tends to come from the heart. Prayer concerns matters that need immediate attention as well as future hopes and dreams.

You may not believe in prayer. Try it for thirty days and if it is not beneficial, stop. Pray out loud together. An easy way to start is to take turns praying one sentence at a time. Pray a sentence for your partner, for each child and for the other parents. Try to be specific. You could ask for help for a child on a test or for a solution to a situation at work. Or you could ask that God help your children's other parents be more reasonable if you are having difficulty with them.

But be careful in your prayers. I have found that when I pray for patience, I find myself facing situations that require patience. A few years ago I was in one of two groups flying to a convention. The groups were leaving from different airports. Both airports were covered in fog. Our group prayed for the fog to lift. We left and arrived on time. The other group prayed for patience and arrived eight hours late. That's when I learned to pray for solutions!

Practice Understanding

Stress! Nobody knows more about stress than a couple who is trying to blend two families. Creating and maintaining a blended family can be exasperatingly stressful. As parents and step-parents we have to manage the children's developing relationships, our relationship with our new step-children, and care for our new partner. Plus we have our own adjusting to do, not to mention the adjustment to our ex's potential for blending another family. Add to this the stress we experience at work and the efforts we make to present our wonderful, blissful new lives to the world, our friends and our relatives. This situation is new, tiring, and sometimes frustrating.

Be aware of the challenges that you and your partner are facing. One of you may be a first-time parent or may be a first time parent of either girls or boys. Perhaps one of you has a teenager for the first time. Boys respond to you differently than girls do. Girls play differently than boys. And we all know that teenagers are a breed all their own! Parenting in this situation while you adjust to living with a new spouse should be in the Webster's dictionary as the definition of stress.

Although you and your partner are experiencing similar emotions, stresses and changes, remember that each of you are facing them as individuals, too. You may be having a good day, while your partner is having a bad day. He may be having a problem with one of your children, or an ex. She may have a problem at work that is compounded when she gets home and has to cook dinner for a variety of people and tastes.

If your partner snaps at you but you haven't done anything wrong, recognize this as a distress signal. Do Not Take It Personally! Your partner has just sent up a flare. Look and listen for the cause of the problem. It is probably not you. It's just that she's lost at sea. And you might just have the life raft. Ask if you can help. Step in and take over a chore or a situation with the children and allow your partner time to decompress. *Ask* what you can do better. *Ask* if there is a better way to handle a situation. Think back over behavior patterns so you can recognize behaviors that can be adjusted or adapted. For instance; Dotti learned quickly not to let me take a nap. From the time I was a child, I have been grumpy when I get up from a nap. My grumpiness has nothing to do with her or the children but with the way an afternoon nap affects me. Dotti quickly learned not to take my grouchy attitude personally but rather to remind me not to go to sleep in the afternoon. I, for my part, try to remember that she has in mind our best interest as a couple when she reminds me to stay awake. It would be easy for me to snap at her and then go to sleep anyway. But the long term results just aren't worth the short nap. I have learned that willingness to discuss my own shortcomings creates an open discussion and helps both of us to understand how the other is feeling and move toward solutions.

Understanding takes effort on your part. When you feel like your partner is complaining or criticizing, listen for the useful information. People typically become defensive when they feel attacked. The natural response is to return complaint for complaint. But, try this: stop before you speak. Take a breath. Review what your partner said and think about it. Try to separate the details and tone from the core message. What is it your partner is saying he or she needs? Problem solving occurs when both partners stay focused on the root of the problem. For instance, if your new spouse accuses you of not helping to motivate the children to help around the house, your response should start with acknowledgment of her feelings, not with a rebuttal of how much you think you have done to motivate the kids. Acknowledging how she feels does not indicate that you necessarily agree with her feelings, but it goes a long way to open up lines of communication. That is the first step toward solving the problem. After acknowledging her feelings, ask her for a possible solution to the problem and then share any solutions you may have. Work together to develop a solution you both can agree on and then implement it. Focus on producing a solution and avoid thinking about how big a problem it is, has been, or might continue to be. The solution is what matters.

Build a Consensus

Every household has a set of unwritten rules that everybody in the house follows. Each member helps to enforce these rules. In a traditional family each member has grown up with these rules. Each person in your blended family comes from a household that had a set of rules. The challenge for the blended family is to develop its own set of rules.

You and your partner are probably used to doing things a little differently as a single parent or in your previous relationships. What do you do when one child hits another? What about when one of them disobeys you? Does homework come before play or do they need some play time to relax before doing homework? You may handle these issues differently than your spouse does. You as a couple will probably have to handle these a little differently than either of you did before you blended your families. Some of the old rules may not work in your larger family. You will have to consider adding some new rules or changing old ones.

It is possible to decide some of the rules ahead of time. Discuss with your partner things like bedtimes and curfews. Do you need rules for sharing bathroom time among girls who once had separate baths? Consider what else will have to be shared now. When are the children allowed to have snacks? What is an acceptable snack? The difficulty here is that you cannot think of everything. We had two children the same age, but their bedtimes were 30 minutes apart. That didn't work. We had to agree on which time we thought was best and change the rule for one of the children.

It will take you and your partner time to build a consensus on how your house will operate. You will build a consensus as you handle the problems or conflicts that arise from the little differences each family member brings with them to your new family. Be willing to change your rules. Remember it isn't a big deal. Your rules will change as your children grow older anyway. Let this be an opportunity for you to model flexibility and wisdom. Remember that you are not changing your rules so much as setting the rules for your new family. As time goes by and you accumulate experiences together, you and your partner will learn to build a consensus on how to parent your children much more easily.

Building consensus means learning how to collaborate to make a decision that meets both persons' expectations to the best or highest degree possible. This process means that when people are in conflict or have a problem to solve they look for ways to combine their different approaches into one approach that meets the most people's needs. Consensus building begins with making sure everyone agrees on what the problem to be solved is. Then the people involved in developing the solution individually write down the steps they feel need to occur to solve the problem. Everyone shares their steps and look for similarities in the lists. Those similarities become the foundation for the collaborative solution. After identifying similarities from each list look for items on the other peoples list that you feel are good ideas. Discuss the pro's and con's of those ideas and then incorporate the ones you can agree on into your solution. Usually by this time a viable solution has been developed and is easily agreed upon by those involved. Now it is time to try the solution and see what happens. If it works…great, if not try it again before adding new ideas or trying a totally new approach.

Household Chores

There can be a lot more work to do in a blended family. More clothes and dishes to wash, more pets to feed and care for, larger meals and more school lunches to prepare. And more homework that needs to be done.

It is too much for one person to do. Both of you need to help get these things done. It would be unfair, overwhelming and probably exhausting for one of you to do it all. You need to share the load so that you will have time and energy for each other.

Have a general discussion of who is or will be responsible for what around the house. This is not a rigid agreement but rather a way of determining the usual manner in which something happens. Things like who is responsible for dinner on Tuesdays, who is going to cut the grass or take out the trash or wash the clothes. This should not be restricted to just you two; decide what duties the children should have as well. You may decide to change your decisions once you put them into practice. It may vary from day to day or week to week. One couple we know holds a sit down family meeting every Sunday evening to plan the week ahead. They limit the meeting to about an hour and schedule the events they know will happen the next week and schedule chore duties. Each person is allowed input into the process. This meeting also allows the children to learn to plan ahead for leisure activities they may want to do with family or friends and to work out the details with parents. Keep trying until you find what works for your family.

Go the Extra Mile

Once you have had this discussion, show your love in your actions by doing what needs to be done when you see it, whether or not it is part of your usual responsibility. The clothes will pile up. Dishes will be stacked all over the kitchen. The yard will need attention. One of you will have to work late. Your relationship with your partner does not hinge upon each carrying an equal load of chores. Your relationship benefits when the little (or not so little) chores are done and you then have time to enjoy one another. Your relationship also benefits if flexibility allows for the chores to not always be done by a specific time.

Guys, this means noticing the small things that need to be done and may mean throwing the clothes in the washing machine and figuring out how to do it without messing it up (Put the whites in by themselves, or maybe the towels. Colors go together, but don't wash them on hot!). Maybe the clothes just need to be folded or the dishes need to be washed or put up. Stop leaving your clothes or papers lying around the house. Put your dirty underwear in the hamper; don't leave them on the bathroom floor. Doing the extra things shows your love for her. Ladies, take out the trash yourself when it is overflowing, feed the dog or cut the grass (its good exercise). Be understanding and appreciate the effort he makes, even when he messes up or does differently than you would have. Both of you remember to thank the other occasionally for doing the normal duties of running a household.

Be patient. It may take a few attempts before your partner

gets it right, but once they do you will appreciate their help. Remember that there are many ways to do a chore. Just because your partner does it differently than you do, doesn't mean it was done improperly.

If you think about it, you probably did these things and a lot more when you were single. Don't stop now. There is too much to do. Doing a little thing now when you have the opportunity will create more time later for you to spend with your partner.

Be the Enforcer

It is important to your partner's position in the family that you respect their authority. When you show respect for your partner's decisions, your children (and theirs) will learn to respect and obey your partner. The children learn that they can trust both of you.

If you do not support your partner, you undermine their authority as a parent. Your children will learn that they do not have to listen to the new stepparent. They will ignore your partner and have little respect for them. If you fail to support or trust your partner with some parental authority over your own children, then they will be reduced to the role of a bystander. You may even turn them into a tattletale. Neither role is pleasant for your partner. Nor will it help them develop a relationship with our children. It can create resentment between the two of you.

When your partner asks one of your children to do something, like take out the trash or turn down the TV, show your support by being the Enforcer. Use your authority to make sure that your partner's request is obeyed. This demonstrates to everyone that your partner has authority in the house. If necessary, make it clear that you expect your children to listen to the new stepparent. Your need to support your partner as the Enforcer will lessen over time. (However, it seems that I have become the Enforcer for the boys and Dotti for the girls. Natural parenthood seems to matter a lot less.) As you enforce each other's authority as a parent, your children will learn to listen and obey both of you.

Give your partner permission, in front of the kids, to parent your children and get the same permission from them to parent theirs. It is important that the children learn they cannot use you against each other in the parenting process. Often newly married couples in a blended family make the mistake of not allowing the stepparent make any parenting decisions for their biological children. This makes it easy for the children to divide and conquer by pitting the parents against each other. Children are designed to test the limits and it is much easier to get away with things if the authority is not consistent.

Disagree in Private

You will not always agree with your partner. Yet it is important that you do not undermine their authority in the house. If you confront your partner publicly (in front of the children), you can set a bad example for the children. You may show that your partner's decisions do not merit respect and do not have to be obeyed.

When you disagree with a decision your partner has made, go have a private discussion. Go back to the bedroom and decide how to handle the situation better. First, be sure you know what happened or the basis used for making the decision. Try not to confront one another but talk about what you didn't like or how it might have been handled differently. Look beyond this one decision by remembering that there will likely be similar situations that will arise in the future. The longer view often helps take some of the urgency out of the present situation and makes it easier to modify the decisions made in the present situation. From time to time, Dotti has shown me that I have over-reacted to an incident. When I have gone back to reduce a sentence or apologize, my position as "Dad of the house" has been enhanced. By discussing this privately, Dotti has allowed me to maintain the position of authority as I change my decision. The children know that she has influenced my decision, but I changed. How would the children view my authority if she came in, said that I was over-reacting and replaced my decision with her own? When you disagree in private, you achieve the same result without harming the position of your partner.

If your partner disagrees with how you have parented their natural children in a particular situation, listen and offer any explanations. Discuss the matter so that you both learn to parent better. But these are their natural children and their decision carries the most weight as does yours with your natural children.

Team Decisions

You can avoid some potential conflict by making decisions as a team. Before you make a decision or change a decision previously made, check with your partner. You may only need to make sure that there are no conflicts on the calendar, but this courtesy builds trust within the family. When you confirm a decision with your partner, you will not have to reverse that decision later and you avoid all the time and effort required to set things right. When you check with your partner, you show your partner that they are important to you.

Sometimes as the new parent, you may be unsure of whether or not to grant a request or how to give appropriate discipline. You want to talk to your partner before proceeding. It may be impossible or impractical to talk with your partner at that moment. Delay your decision. In most situations it is possible to wait for your partner to be available. We have delayed decisions regarding children going to the movies or to spend the night with a friend. The waits are usually not long and the benefits of team decisions outweigh the frustration of having to wait.

Sometimes, you (or your child) just can't wait. You are the parent. Make the best decision you can. Whether your partner agrees with your decision or not, this will be a part of the consensus building process. When you discuss the decision later, be open to learning so that you will know what you and your partner will want in future similar situations. Remember to reverse the roles and ask what your partner would do if they were in your position. Decide how you as a team want to resolve the situations in the future. There probably won't be much of a discussion if your partner agrees with your decision, and you learn more when your partner disagrees. You can limit the number of things you need to discuss when you talk every day. A lot of these matters relate to the calendar. If you discuss your family calendar, both of you will know not to allow the child with an afternoon activity, like the dentist, practice, or a haircut, to go to the movies. It is important to have a central family calendar where events can be written down. This calendar can be placed in a central location of the house or on the Internet. Anywhere that any family member can have access and can add to or detract from scheduled events. It is important to look at the calendar daily to stay updated with changes as they occur.

One other advantage of team decision making is that the children know that we discuss them and that we make decisions together. This knowledge enhances our individual authority as parents. The children know that when either of us speaks, we speak for both of us.

41

Couple Time

One of the major challenges of raising a blended family is that of finding time to spend alone with your partner. We need to devote time to this relationship so that it develops into the lifelong union that we desire. Failure to care for our relationship with our partner can lead to its demise.

The challenge is that in a blended family time is in short supply. Work and the children also require our time. We must take advantage of the opportunities we have to spend time together as they arise. That alone is not enough because it often means that we give our couple relationship infrequent and sporadic attention. Worse those opportunities come when we are exhausted from caring for all our other responsibilities. Your relationship will not thrive under these circumstances.

The answer is to schedule time together. When you schedule a time to be together, you have time to renew your energy and to reflect on how well you're doing. You have time for serious discussions and time to relax, rest and do the things you enjoy together. If your situation provides you with times during which you have no children, you will find this to be an advantage to your relationship and to your family. It is far easier for you and your partner to have the time and space you need to adjust to your new blended family roles and to one another. If you are not this fortunate, you can plan ahead and make this a priority.

Date Night : One way to create some couple time is to have a date night. Get a sitter and see a movie and/ or get dinner. If you can't afford a sitter, then trade the kids with a neighbor or friends, or pool the kids and share a sitter. Plan a date night at home after all the kids are in bed. Prepare a special dinner, turn down the lights and have a favorite refreshment. Play a game. Rent a movie or watch one on TV. Take a walk around the neighborhood together (This also works for time alone separately.) Set aside a special time on your calendar as a regular event and keep the appointment. Do this once a week. Even if you can only find one hour, you will find it to be very valuable.

Supper Club : The couple time you spend with your partner should include time with other couples. When you include other couples in your plans, you will discover that your life and the way it works is not so unusual. That can be encouraging.

One way to create time with other couples (and a regular date night) is to start a supper club. A Supper club is a group of friends who meet for supper on a regular basis. It is usually four or more couples. Some clubs meet as often as once a month. We found that meeting every six weeks works best for us.

You can meet at different restaurants or rotate to the home of each couple. Usually the host couple will provide the main course and the others the rest of the meal. Although one of our favorites is "steak night," where each couple brings their own steaks for the grill. You will soon find that you really don't meet for the food, it's the company that matters.

We began our supper club by asking a few couples over for a cup of coffee and told them that we were interested in beginning a supper club. Some of the couples did not know each other before we began our club. Over the years we have lost three couples and added two. The interested couples came and we got the calendar to set a date for each couple to be the host. The host couple calls the rest a week or so ahead and organizes the dinner. We have had different food theme nights like, Mexican and German. One host asked everyone to bring their favorite bottle of wine and we had a wine tasting. Your group will have some great ideas too. If supper club sounds like too much work try starting a dessert club. David and his wife Celly are active in a dessert club that reduces the work involved with a typical supper club. The host makes or buys a couple of desserts and invites the participants over around 8:00 p.m. Couples bring their own beverage and the host couple has a couple of board games conducive to 6 or more players. Usually the men challenge the girls to games like Scattagories, Balderdash, Taboo, etc.. This club is very easy going and they have a lot of fun without a lot of work. Decide which type of club you are interested in and make your list and start calling.

Let's Do Lunch: Or breakfast. If your kids are in school create some couple time by meeting for lunch. Do not invite co-workers or friends. You can meet at a restaurant, in the cafeteria at work or take a bag lunch and eat in a convenient park or on the business grounds.

If your work schedules are different, you may be able to meet on one of the lunch breaks. It may be that you can meet every day, once a week, or only when one of you has a day off and the other doesn't. You may meet for breakfast as one of you is heading home and the other is going in to work. Make it happen.

Take a Coffee Break: On Saturday mornings, we often take a coffee break. We settle the kids, then we take our coffee and morning paper into our seldom used living room. Amazingly, the kids seem to get along without us for a while. They seem to forget where we are. We are out of sight and out of mind.

This creates a small window of couple time for us. Sometimes we share the comics and other things that catch our attention. Sometimes we just listen to the children or the sounds of the house. If you don't have a living room, pick another room. The bedroom and our deck are also favorite break areas. Don't limit your break times to breakfast. You can take a break any time of day. Sometimes you will only be able to find a few minutes, but you may get an hour.

Buy a Book: Go to the bookstore and spend some time picking out some resources that will help to keep the spark and fun in your relationship alive. Most of the major bookstores have an entire section devoted to books about building couple relationships. David believes strongly that he does not have all the answers to all of the issues that arise in a relationship. It is important to seek the wisdom of others to gain useful ideas and knowledge. Books are often full of useful information. The time spent looking for a useful book for your relationship can turn into quality discussion, fun and quality time.

Time Away

Blending a family is tiring and stressful, especially in the first few years. While couple time will give us most of the opportunity we need to decompress, we all need some individual time away from the family. This can be time alone or with friends. It doesn't have to be long. Thirty minutes alone can be wonderful.

Time away probably doesn't need to be put into your schedule like couple time. You should both be sure that the other takes reasonable advantage of the opportunity for time away. Remember that while you are away your partner is not. It can be a good idea to plan some time away so that it is back to back. One of you returns refreshed so that the other can begin their time away.

You can find time away when you send your partner on a walk around the block. Guard the bathroom door while she takes a long, hot bath. Send your partner to play golf or cards or to have coffee with a friend. Or shopping. Even going to the grocery store without kids can be a treat. No money? Window shopping can be fun or test driving a dream car. If finances allow, surprise your partner with a gift certificate for a massage, tennis lesson or a session at the tanning salon.

Quality Time

The amount of time demanded by your children and other obligations (work) will limit the amount of time you can spend with your partner. This can lead to a neglect of your relationship with your partner or to a tendency to over-plan how you spend your time together in an effort to create "quality time." Quality time is time that is meaningful. It is difficult to know whether we spent quality time until we view it from our memory. It seems to me that quality times are the good things we remember. These memories include specific events and detail but they also include less specific memories of how we did things and how we lived. I do not recall a lot of specific conversation or events from our Saturday morning coffee breaks. But I do recall sitting close together, laughing and smiling. The memories of our coffee breaks keep me warm. These are quality times.

Creating quality time on demand is very difficult. You will find that quality time springs unexpectedly from quantity time. In a blended family quantity time is also very difficult. Quality time will often come from the stolen times you create. It will appear during the surprise coffee break visit, the quick lunch or the extra cup of coffee on a Saturday morning. Date nights are a treasured source of quality time. You may not recognize these times for the quality they provide while you are experiencing them, but when you look back they form a marvelous background for your love.

Finances Matter

One of the most important areas of blending a family is often the most overlooked issue when joining families together. Many couples assume that their new partner handles finances in similar ways that they do prior to getting remarried. It is easy to forget that one of the most often fought about issue in any marriage is the financial aspect of running a family. Due to the added financial issues of child-support, alimony, and just the expense of adding more children into the family mix, many couples that create a blended family head for early marital problems because they have not recognized the financial issues they may face. Issues surrounding "my money" and "your money" and "our money" can become veritable land mines for the new marital and family relationships. Children will often add stress and pressure to all parents involved because the divorce will create a change in their financial lifestyles and they will learn how to manipulate any area of division between all parents involved. Ex spouses and new spouses can get territorial over money issues and arguments of who pays for what child's expenses will often create opportunity for major conflicts in the new marriage.

The best way to handle this issue is to work together to form a financial plan and budget that will work best for all involved. It is essential that a budget be developed that both partners can contribute to and agree to pay the current household expenses. If you have different financial styles it is important that you begin early working together and having weekly or even daily conversations about the finances. The more financially responsible partner cannot let the person who does not watch their spending get off the hook with a "I'm just not good at it" or "Finances scare me" kind of attitude. The best method of managing household finances is to work together to stick to a budget that will keep a lid on over-spending and a focus on appropriate saving.

Often in the case of blending a family one partner comes into the second marriage with more assets and money than the other. Issues of retirement, college educations and inheritances have to be discussed, agreed upon and planned for. Seek financial advice from professionals early to know the best way to protect assets and save money for both sets of children.

Other ideas to incorporate into the financial plan include forming unified goals and plans for saving, spending and earning money. Develop a savings plan that allows for college savings and retirement savings. Use cash and avoid credit cards as this can create 15% less in spending. Avoid bringing financial baggage from your old relationship into your new marriage. When you argue about money make sure that you are dealing with current issues not issues from your past marriage. Always tell your partner the truth about spending and finances. Be open about financial conversations with your Ex to your current spouse especially when it deals with your children's needs.

Conclusion

Use these ideas to build a strong love relationship with your partner. Change them as you need to better fit your life. In the next section we will look at raising the children. You cannot put both the children and your relationship with your partner first. Plan and schedule your date night and other time with your partner. Make those a priority. When these times conflict with sudden changes in the children's schedule, you will usually put the children first. You should do that. The children will not always pre-empt your plans. Despite the occasional interruption, you will have the times you will come to treasure as a couple.

Section Two
Raising the Kids

The number one fear or concern of couples beginning to create their own blended family is that of raising the kids. This fear is of the unknown. We don't know how our children will react to having our new partner living in the house. We don't know how our new partner will interact with our children. Can we be a parent to our partner's children? How will our partner's children respond to us? How will the children get along together?

You and your partner may have had a wonderful relationship with the children while you were dating. IT is different when some or all of you are living in the same house. There is a difference between a playmate that comes to visit occasionally and a step-brother/sister who is getting a bedroom of their own or sharing one with you. The authority and responsibility of a parent's girl/boyfriend can be very different from that exercised by a new stepparent.

A second major concern is time. Now that you are together the word "hectic" can take on a completely new meaning. Just keeping ahead of things can be tough. And now each set of children of your children belongs to two households. That means you will have to keep up with the schedule for three households. Each of those households has different and sometimes conflicting events that involve important members of that household. There will, of course, be events that involve your children. Other events that concern grandparents, cousins, other step or half siblings and the other parents are important to your children. And don't forget how the holidays will impact your schedule!

It is enough to begin to question your sanity. You will find that there is enough time to do the important things. Occasionally, you may have to put off cutting the grass and a bed or two may not get made in the morning. Sometimes your days will not go as planned. You had these days before you decided to blend your family. Now you are not alone. Your partner can help you do all the car-pooling and errand running that as a single parent you did all by yourself. You may even have an extra set of grandparents to assist as well. Now you can be in two places at once if you ask and receive the extra help that another parent living in the house can provide.

For all the fears and worries that come with blending a family, there are also more privileges. We often like to talk about how hard it is to raise children. They are loud, messy and they sometimes don't listen. They also provide us with wonderful memories and great joys that we can hardly describe. We share their pride and excitement when they succeed and their sorrow when their feelings are hurt. In a blended family, you get the privilege of sharing these times with children that were not born to you. It is often a privilege that their other parent will never have an opportunity to experience. Whether you helped on the big school project that got an "A," or helped coach the basketball team or merely endured the practices for the piano recital, you'll be proud and jubilant when your child succeeds. You won't care if they are one of your natural children or not.

As you start to blend your family, there are two factors that are beyond your control. First, you cannot control the ages of the children. Younger children need adult involvement in their lives. They, therefore, tend to be more accepting of a stepparent. Pre teens and teenagers are beginning to be more independent. They want less and less parental involvement and may have more difficulty accepting a stepparent. This factor is not directed at you personally, but more a part of the child's growing independence. Second, you cannot control the amount of time the children spend in your home. Some type of legal proceeding has usually set the amount of time. Obviously, the more time you spend with someone, the more opportunity you have to grow closer. The relationship you create with a teenager who lives most of the time with their other parent will be very different from the one you create with a two year old who lives in your home. Rather, your relationship will develop differently. Remember, too, that the children really didn't get to choose you. So, what do you do to help blend your family successfully?

Be a Parent to All the Children

How do you handle your new children when you first get remarried? You have entered into a household that is new to everybody. You may not know your children very well nor they you. We all know that it takes time for any relationship to grow. So, what do you do in the meantime?

Act like a parent. When you begin your blended family, the parent/child order is in place. You have a position of authority in the house. It is the extent of your authority that has often not been settled.

There are two kinds of parental authority to be established. One is that of a leader of a house. Under this authority you make decisions, grant or deny permissions and are the disciplinarian. The second kind of authority is that of caregiver. Under this authority you give comfort and assistance.

You may even wonder if you have the authority to ask the children to straighten a room or to take out the trash. Because you are the (new) spouse, you are the "Mom" or "Dad" of this house. You do have the authority and even the responsibility. Assume the authority that goes with the position. When you assume the authority, it will usually be given to you.

When you act like a parent, the children will respond to you as a parent. Both you and the children know what a parent does and how a parent acts. The roles are familiar to you and your new children. (If you are a first time parent, see the next section.) That means that when the children don't listen or obey, it is most often the children behaving like children and not a personal challenge to your new position. Even if it is a challenge to your new position the way you handle this early will help determine your effectiveness as a parental figure in the household. This does not mean you have to handle it like a drill sergeant, but you do need to be firm, caring and consistent.

Be involved with your new children just as you have with your own children. The difference is you have to be active in seeking the involvement. Involvement means being willing to spend time with them and to communicate *with* them. Be available to them. Stop what you are doing and help them with their homework, chores, or personal problems. Talk to and listen to them.

While that sounds good, it is not always easy. You may find it a bit awkward. Your new children will not come to you first. They will usually wait for their natural parent to be available. They will often refuse your help. Keep offering anyway. Remember that in a new situation we all tend to favor those things that are familiar and comfortable. In a new blended family, children will want their natural parent first and parents often seek out their own children first. Support your partner by encouraging your children to accept your partner's offers of help and involvement. Encourage your partner to keep trying with your children.

Model Behavior

If you are beginning a blended family and you have never been a parent before, you may be scared. You may believe that you don't know what a parent does or how to live with children. Do not be afraid. You do know how to be a parent as well as any parent of a first baby. After all you have experience being parented and you have learned many skills from this past experience. You learned both what and what not to do. That is all that is required. As a first time parent you will not have to face the challenges of blending two sets of children right away therefore you have the advantage of practicing with your new step-children.

You know how a parent behaves from your own parents and from watching other parents. You have watched your new partner parent your new children while you were dating. You can model or copy those parents and can focus on the skills you thought were positive and especially effective. This is what all new parents do.

There are several other models you can follow. You don't have to have a love relationship with the children to be the adult in the house. You are one of the adults and not the friend or the playmate. You can be the friendly adult, but not the "pal" or "buddy." You can control the outer boundaries of what is permissible, while allowing the children to make decisions within those boundaries.

You can be like an active baby sitter or a nanny. Not one that only watches and prevents disaster. If your neighbor left their child with you for an afternoon, you would exercise control over that child. You would tell them to turn down the TV or ask them to put something back in its place. You might involve them in an activity like coloring a picture or playing a game. You may or may not participate. Do this with your new children. Give directions firmly and in a caring manner. Be willing to follow through with your directions by setting limits on the children that are age appropriate. Learn how to never have to say no by offering alternative choices to requests that you feel are inappropriate or you are unable to fulfill.

Another model to learn from would be that of a schoolteacher or day care worker. They are responsible for the children while they have them. They expect the children to listen and obey them. And, for the most part, the children do.

The ultimate source of a baby-sitter's or teacher's authority is the child's natural parent. Your authority comes from the same source. You have been given authority by your partner by simply being made a part of the family. Your children usually understand this, however it is often effective if they hear your partner give you this authority in front of them. This will help deflect the "You're not my parent" response if their natural parent has given you this authority formally. The children will respond to that authority while your relationship is growing.

Be Flexible and Unselfish

Raising a blended family requires that your children and stepchildren have a high level of trust in you. In order to create that trust, you must put your all of your children first directly behind your relationship with your partner. That means you must be flexible and unselfish. Being flexible means that you will have to be able to change your plans quickly. Sometimes literally at a moment's notice. Unselfishness means putting your children ahead of your plans and your feelings about your ex.

This really isn't anything new. But you must show the children that they can still depend on you in this new situation. Your stepchildren want to learn if they can depend on you as well.

There will be times when you have to skip an evening out or a game of golf, bowling or tennis. You may have to be late to an event or dinner out with friends. What do you do when you "get invited" to take pre-dance pictures thirty minutes ahead of time because the other parent had a sudden unexplained conflict? You re-arrange your schedule and go take some great pictures.

We learned this lesson on our wedding night. After we were married on a November Sunday afternoon, we went to our house before leaving for a short honeymoon. We got a phone call shortly after we got home. Two of our children had left their coats at the reception hall about twenty minutes away. In order to get the coats back to where they were needed, we spent a part of our wedding night with each of our new mother's in law and my ex. This was not how we planned to make our wedding night memorable, but memorable it was.

You're Not My Mom/Dad

As a parent in your blended family, you do have parental authority. The extent of your authority can only be established in day-to-day experience. Your authority will soon be tested. Your authority will be tested when a stepchild first says, "You're not my Mom/Dad!"

This challenge will come in response to some instruction given or in response to your efforts to help or comfort. Recognize that this challenge is being used because of the likelihood that it will work on you. Were the child's natural parent in your position a different challenge would have been used. One of our children has always tried to push the limits. I can see now that he does it with everybody, but at first I took it personally. All children will try to expand their boundaries and challenge parental authority in the process of growing up. Your tendency will be to be more sensitive to challenges from your new children, but all the children will do it at some point in time.

Handle the "you're not my Mom/Dad" challenge by first acknowledging that the statement is true. Then you must demonstrate that the statement is irrelevant. If your authority as leader is being challenged, remind the child that you are the Mom/Dad of this house. If necessary, ask your partner for support. Strongly support your partner when it happens to them. If your authority as a caregiver is being challenged, again admit the truth of the statement and then remind the child that you care about them too and you can help. If you *appear* calm and follow through with the truth, this challenge will soon disappear. The challenge will disappear because it will not work.

I Want to Live with Mom/Dad!

This is a very different challenge from "You're not my Mom/Dad!" It is targeted at both the natural parent and the stepparent. It can be either a challenge to your authority or a serious request. The circumstances that prompt the statement will help determine the seriousness of the request.

First, do not take the request personally. Whether this comes as a challenge or a request, your child is appearing to reject you. This is not an indication that you have somehow failed as a parent. Your relationship with your child is not being terminated, they mainly disagree with the way you are parenting them. This is not to say that you are doing anything wrong, they just have a different perspective than you do.

In order to handle this issue properly, you will have to be open to the possibility that living with the other parent may be best for your child. You don't have to like the idea. You can oppose it. But you must be willing to honestly discuss the issue with your child.

If this issue arises as a challenge to your authority, you will want to defuse it. You will recognize it as a challenge because the issue will arise in response to a request you have made, permission you have denied, or a punishment you have issued. The purpose of the remark is to make you change a decision. You can take all the power out of "I want to live with my Dad/ Mom" by offering to discuss the issue after the task you have set out is complete when the punishment is finished or when the child is no longer angry over your decision. Require that the child come to you to discuss the issue. Make sure that the child understands that you don't want them to leave but you always want what us best for them and you are willing to discuss it with them. The power of this statement when it is used as a challenge comes from your fear of losing your child or fear that they want or like their other parent more than you. You defuse the statement when you show that you are not afraid by being willing to discuss and consider it for the right reasons.

If this issue comes as a genuine request, you and your partner should take time to privately discuss it with your child. Ask them why. Be gentle and be reassuring that you are not offended by the request. Be willing to discuss the pro's and con's for all involved: you, your mate, your child and your ex and their mate. Again, you truly want what is best for your child. Examine yourselves to see if there are things that you need to change. Just because a child asks to live with their other parent does not mean it will happen. It may only be a way to begin a discussion of an issue that can be resolved.

If you find that it really is in the best interests of your child to live with their other parent, make the transaction as smooth as possible. Reassure your child of your continued love. Talk with them often after the move.

You should treat a request to come live with you in a similar way. In many cases a change of households isn't going to solve the child's difficulties anyway. A child may not see that you will require them to do their homework and to keep their room clean because they don't have weekend homework and your weekend rules are more relaxed than the weekday rules they now follow. They may get the impression that one parent is easier to live with based upon when they visit. Take the time to discover the real reason for your child's request.

Also, avoid threatening to send your child to live with their other parent. Although is may work for a while, there are dangers here. This could affect self-esteem issues for the child. This is an indirect criticism of the child's other parent. It says "You are being a bad kid so I am going to really punish you by sending you to live with your good for nothing parent." And another problem with a threat happens when the child responds with "Great, I can't wait to go!" or "Great, when do I leave?" If you are having problems with your children when they are in your home it is up to you as a parent to find ways to confront the problem healthily.

Talk with Your Kids

You know you need to discover what is happening in you children's lives. Talk with your children to monitor how they are adjusting to the blended family. Talking with (all) of your children about the blended family gives your children an avenue to share their feelings. You are able to help them by offering explanations or possible solutions. Sometimes you'll see that they simply need reassurance or a hug. The important issue is that all of your children feel comfortable talking about the way they feel without being punished for it.

Encourage the children to talk to you by asking about their friends. Discover what they like or don't like at school. It is very important to ask good questions and then to listen to their answers. Good questions ask for a story or require an explanation or description. Good questions ask for more detail. Good questions avoid the child being able to respond with just a yes, no, or O.K..

Once you have asked a good question, you need to listen carefully. Listening involves more than hearing. Watch how your child responds. Listen to the feeling behind the response. Is there sadness, happiness, worry, joy, or frustration? Listening for the feelings will help you to know whether you need to probe further. You aren't seeking a soul-bearing conversation everyday. You just want to know that they're adjusting well.

Some children love to talk. Some don't. Your new children may be a little hesitant to share their feelings with you at first. Don't be discouraged. Keep trying. Remember that there are differences between boys and girls and between children of different ages. All of our girls love to talk to you. One of our boys will give you details only if you ask specifically. With him you have to ask " Who did you play with at recess today?" and continue with direct questions. With the others this question brings at least a five-minute response. Even our talkers don't feel like talking some days. They may be on the way to the computer or X-box, a favorite show may be starting, or a friend may be waiting outside. Try again later.

Use open-ended questions to start your conversation. Questions like "What did you do that was fun today?" and "Who did you play with at recess?" and "What was the best thing that happened to you today?" will usually bring a response you can develop into a conversation. If you get the "nothing" or "nobody" response, try asking a question that gives you a yes or no response and work from there. Then retry the open-ended questions again.

You also should talk to your children to get the information you need about their schedules. Don't forget to talk to your children about the plans their other parent has for them. This is not being nosy. It helps co-ordinate your plans with the other parent. Often this information will alert you to ask the other parent about an upcoming event or weekend trip. It will reduce the likelihood of learning about a change of plans at the last minute. The more information each household has about plans involving the children, the easier it is for us to make any necessary adjustments.

Sometimes talking is not enough. You will find that a monthly calendar to post upcoming events to be very helpful. Copies of school calendars and game schedules can be posted in a common area to be visible by all. Coordinating your schedule with your ex has many advantages when parenting your children. Offer to share your calendar of parenting events with your ex and ask them to share theirs with you as a means of coordinating parenting plans more effectively.

A regular place to leave a note or write-on board can be helpful when someone had gone across the street or to the store. It is always good to give the children an avenue in which to let the parents know where they are. As they get old enough and mature enough use of a cell phone can come in handy for coordinating plans or changes in plans.

Special Talks

When the time comes to talk to a child about sex, drugs, or any other serious issue, do not assume that the other parent has talked to them. Even if the other parent has primary custody, you should make sure that these talks occur with your children. It is optimal if you discuss your plans to have these talks with your ex prior to doing so in order to come to an agreement of the best age or time to do so. If you cannot come to an agreement then you will have to do what you think is best. If the other parent has not had this talk, you will be sharing important information. If your child should have two talks about these subjects, so much the better. Your child will have had a chance to answer all of their questions and clarify any confusion they have made. When Dotti began to have a talk with our oldest daughter, Dotti learned that our daughter had already had the talk three times: her natural mother, her grandfather, and me. They still talked.

Problems can arise when a Stepparent with good intentions talks with a stepchild about sensitive topics without discussing it with the natural parents first. It is important that the natural parent have the first opportunity to have these talks with their children. Stepparents should have these talks in conjunction with the natural parent. Discuss with your partner and decide how you want to handle these matters.

Be Fair

Be fair to all your children. Being fair in a blended family does not always mean spending equal dollars or equal time on each child. While there is an aspect of equality, most often being fair requires that you recognize and meet the needs of each individual child.

Each child will have somewhat different needs. Some will have more trouble adjusting to the blended family than others. Some will need more help with their homework. Sometimes one will need some attention after a tough day at school. The needs of your children will differ from day-to-day.

As you begin blending your family the needs of all your children will be high. They will want your attention. They will want to be reassured. They will be dealing with uncertainty and change. This can get better quickly. When we first began, one sure way to get attention from one of my natural daughters was for me to give attention to one of my stepchildren. This usually resulted in a group hug.

Be lavish with your hugs, kisses, and attention. Include all the children. Play a game with a group of your children or watch a show. If you are involved in a project, invite them to help. When you are fair with your children by meeting their needs, you will not usually need to watch the clock or measure dollars.

Being fair does include some equality. Inequality will often appear as favoritism. It can be easy to favor your natural children without recognizing it. You may also favor the children who live with you over those who visit. Favoritism will only create jealousies and tensions among the children. It can even cause resentment in your partner. Check with each other to be sure that you are being fair to all.

Allow Time and Space

Whenever we face significant change, it takes time for us to become adjusted to the change. Our emotions may become volatile. We need space to express emotions, if only to vent some steam. Everyone in the family should have the ability to find some personal time and space within the household.

In a new blended family, our children need the same time and space to adjust to the changes. Not only are they experiencing changes in their daily routine, they are also seeking to establish their place in the family. They may also be adjusting to a new house, school, or town.

Try to keep your daily blended family routine as much as like your old routine as possible. This familiarity is comforting to your children, especially younger children. With those things you must change, make it exciting for younger children and point out the benefits for the older one. Mix in some favorite things. If you need to get up earlier to get to school, add a favorite breakfast food to make the change easier to accept.

Your children are also establishing their place in the blended family. You may have a child who is the oldest in one household but becomes a middle child in your new family. Or the youngest child becomes the middle child. You may have a child who has never had a brother/sister before. Learning new roles can be very stressful.

Don't rush the children. My two daughters were frightened by the physical play of their two new brothers. Soon they came to see that's the way boys often play. When Dotti and I first got married, our children insisted on separate weekends. My children spent the weekend with their mother while Dotti's children were with us and vice versa. The children were together one afternoon each week and about one weekend every three months for our first year. We also all went on vacation together. After about a year and one half, the children began to ask to be at our house on the same weekend. My youngest natural daughter enjoys being an older sister at our house, except when she is being tormented by her younger sister. The new middle daughter has gained a new point of view that has had an impact on her relationship with her older (natural) sister.

All of this change and adjusting will cause emotional stress in all the children. They will have their feelings hurt by their siblings. They will be jealous. They will be scared. Don't judge their feelings. These are natural, common emotions.

Give them space or an outlet for their emotions by listening. Help them sort through their emotions by asking questions. For example, "Do you like being an older sister?" . "Aren't little brothers a pain?", or "Big sisters are cool, aren't they?" . Get their answers and point out the positives and negatives. If your new partner was in a similar family position (middle brother, for example), invite your partner to tell about the good and the bad of being the little or big sister/brother. When you give your children space to share their feelings and time to establish their place in the family, they can adjust very well.

Different Rules/Different Times

It may be necessary to have a set of rules in your house for weekends and other times of visitation that are different from your weekday rules. The make-up of your household is different. You may have different ages and genders. You probably have children sharing bedrooms on weekends that are theirs alone during the week.

You need a different set of rules because the situation is different. What is permissible for a child in a private bedroom (loud music, using the entire floor to play with her dolls) will need to be adjusted when the room is shared. You may allow snacks to be taken out of the kitchen during the week but not allow it on weekends because of the volume.

When dealing with these different times, fairness becomes an issue. Is the bedroom more one child's the other's? Who picks up the toys left by both when one has left for the week? It is home to both. We set aside a place in the bedroom for the child that is here less time. In effect, the bedroom is always shared. If we fail to be sure that the room is straight before the visitation is over, we help pick up the toys.

How do you fairly discipline a child that is only home for the weekend? Obviously discipline that might last several days, like restrictions on the TV or computer games won't work. Disciplines that must wait for the next visitation are not as effective. Your discipline needs to be immediate and of short duration. In order to be fair, discipline all the children (as necessary) in a similar fashion. Don't carry a punishment into the week for a child who lives with you when you cannot do the same for another child.

71

Should your visiting children get more time and attention on weekends because you have so little time with them, or is it fair to deny weekend time to the children who are with you during the week? As we've said earlier, being fair does not demand you spend equal time with each child. Give all of your children some time. Include all the children by taking advantage of opportunities for group activities. Take everyone to a sibling's ball games on Saturday morning. Watch some cartoons together after breakfast. Let everyone help wash the cars or rake leaves. There will be time for individual attention too. Despite our hectic schedules, there are usually several times each weekend that I find myself alone with each child as we go about our regular activities. Give them a hug or a high five and ask a question. We don't usually single out any child or group of children for special attention just because of visitation.

How to Manage Disrespectful Teenagers

Teenagers...who in their right mind would want to be one again? Parents of teenagers—none of *us* feel *we* are sane. Handling Teenagers appropriately with all of the issues and concerns that face them in today's society is one of the biggest parenting challenges. This article will give some helpful information on how to deal with teens that are being disrespectful to parents.

The first tip is to keep perspective. Remember your teenager believes that the whole world revolves around them and their world. They do not have the full perspective that you —the adult—has, because of your years of experience. Be careful not to get pulled into a lack of perspective because of what your teen says or does that look and feel disrespectful. Many times the disrespect the teen exhibits is out of their feeling frustrated or powerless to change a decision you are making about their lives. They exhibit this behavior as a means of getting you into a longer argument or discussion in hopes that they may end up changing your mind. Other reasons for the disrespect include displaying their personal power in an effort to save face, to get you to feel powerless or hurt because they feel you have done the same to them, and as a way of trying to exert control in a situation.

The best response to minor disrespect is ignoring it. Any attention a teen receives for behavior is reinforcing. If they are mildly disrespectful (i.e.—rolling eyes, mumbling under their breath as they walk away, stomping up the stairs) giving this any attention tells them they have power to control your feelings and response—therefore the will use this over and over again. If these types of behavior are ignored long enough they will go away or they will no longer have the power to upset you.

The best response to moderate (raised voice, surely attitude, inappropriate faces or gestures) disrespect is to simply state that you will not listen or respond to anyone who is being disrespectful. Once this is said if the teen continues to be mildly to moderately disrespectful—leave the room, stop listening and do not respond to their attention seeking attempts. Let them know you will talk with them when they are ready to do so in a respectful manner and that you will make decisions only after a respectful conversation. It is important to stick to what you say you are going to do!

A good response to extreme disrespect (cursing, bad language, yelling, threatening, breaking things) is to simply state that a rule has been broken and the consequence for breaking the rule. For example: Oops you broke our rule about cussing at your parents therefore you have lost phone privileges for 24 hours—if you continue to be disrespectful then I will not continue this conversation until such time you are willing to do so appropriately. If they continue to be disrespectful walk away without responding to anything else they say. If the behavior escalates and they break another rule let them know they have done so and tell them the consequence for that and tell them that their behavior will decide if they are going to earn more consequences or not. Do not go into a lecture about why they should be respectful or how you would have been treated if you talked to your parents that way etc—because this does not work.

It is important that both parents agree on how to handle the disrespect and that they support each other's parenting decisions. Parents should talk together and decide some of the consequences of disrespect ahead of time and let the children know what to expect when exhibiting disrespectful behavior. Remember—keep your perspective, stay cool, and do not reinforce negative behavior with too much energy or attention.

Holidays

Christmas, Hanukkah, Thanksgiving and the 4th of July are wonderful family holidays. You may have some special family events centered around other times. For some these are the only time of the year that they get to see distance relatives. Yet these holiday times can be the most stressful our children.

If our children weren't getting presents everywhere they went, their holiday schedules might be considered cruel. Consider that over a short holiday each set of your children may be scheduled to see both sets of their parents and up to four sets of grandparents along with a mix of aunts, uncles and cousins that your children may or may not know. Don't forget that your children have a non-stop travel schedule to see all these people. Combined with the general excitement of the holiday, this is enough to exhaust anyone. And then we expect them to be polite and behave.

Be flexible enough to allow time in your schedule for a break for the children to relax and rest. Say no to some of the requests for time or simply tell your relative that you will be late. Everybody cannot have all of us over for every holiday meal. We rotate from holiday to holiday and year to year.

Many of our relatives and friends did not understand our children's holiday schedules. After we explained it to them, our relatives and friends were able to be more flexible with us. Sometimes you can plan to celebrate the holiday with family or friends a day or two before or after the holiday. When we have celebrated on a different day, we have found these times to be very enjoyable. We have more time to spend and our blended family is less tired and less stressed. It can actually be better than a hurried visit on the holiday. Sometimes families get too hung up about having us over on the day of the holiday when it is the spirit of the holiday that is important. Who says we cannot celebrate Christmas more than one day a year, after all there is a song about "The Twelve Days of Christmas" isn't there?

Criticizing the Other Parent

All families, especially blended families, need openness and trust among its members. You want to create a family atmosphere that will allow your children to be open and honest with you. One way to foster this kind of atmosphere is to follow this rule: Do not criticize a child's parent in front of any of the children. Follow this rule even if the other parent doesn't follow it. The effort is very worthwhile.

When you refuse to criticize the other parent in front of your children, you create freedom in your children. They know that they can talk to you about their other parent and what happens in that household with out fear of us condemning some action of the other parent. This allows us to share more fully in their joys and achievements and their bumps and bruises that occur there. If we regularly criticize or question the actions of their other parent, our children will become more guarded in what they share with us. They will be tempted to paint their other parent in a better light. They also may learn to use this opportunity to manipulate us by using our expressed negative feelings to divide and conquer. When you do not criticize, your children learn that they can trust you with the truth and that you will be responsible with it. When your children trust you, they will tell you everything that goes on, good or bad.

This rule can difficult to follow. Our emotions may get the better of us. A child may walk into the room, when we are saying something to our partner. (It is perfectly O.K. to criticize the other parent privately with your partner.) You don't like for anyone to criticize someone you love, even if the criticism is correct. Your children don't either. When you slip-up, apologize. Be careful not to slip-up a lot.

If the child's other parent has obvious problems or habits that the children are aware of, be very strict with the truth. Do not make it worse or better than it is. If, for instance the other parent is a smoker or is constantly late, you may be unable to avoid what appears to be criticism. Talk with your children about their thoughts and feelings on the issue but be careful not to do it in a way that forces the children to feel they are tattling. This can be done by generally discussing their feelings about smoking or being late. Often if you open the door to the topic they will fill it in with the details about how they feel about people in their lives that may have those habits. If necessary, point out that this habit does not make the other parent a bad parent or love the children less.

If you are in a situation which the other parent does not follow this rule, you will soon see that your children will tend to believe you more than their other parent. Your children will come to trust and rely upon your judgement. On the other hand, you will find that consistent unfair criticism of the other parent (or of you) will be discovered to be untrue and can work to undermine the relationship with the children.

Our willingness not to criticize the other parent has often stood in stark contrast to what our other parents have said about us. That may be why this has been so effective for us. Our children seem to have recognized that when we deal with their other parent we are concerned first about their well being and not about continuing battles that should have ended long ago. Imagine how much the children will benefit if both sets of parents make this rule a part of their lives.

Carry this rule over to friends and family. Don't let them

criticize your other parents in front of the children. Your children may see you as agreeing with the criticism and that can hurt too. Our practice has been to tell family and friends that we would rather talk about something more pleasant than our other parents or to simply say that we are uncomfortable talking about certain issues in front of our children.

Create Blended Family Memories

Creating blended family memories helps develop and reinforce the feeling a family for our children and us. A blended family memory is that event or group of events that your family experienced together and recall with one another. These remembered experiences bind us together. These experiences give our blended family a unique identity.

The truth is that you cannot create blended family memories. You can create the opportunity for these memories to be made. The family memories that come from these opportunities will often be unexpected.

Create opportunities by planning a family event. Our kids love to go to any Japanese Steak House because of the show. We take everyone to the movies and share the popcorn. You can plan a picnic, a day at the fair, circus, or zoo.

Vacations are a great way to create blended family memories. The event itself becomes a family memory. The children will grow closer to one another as they experience the trip together. While traveling, the children will tend to hang together because they are more familiar with one another than with the new surroundings. These times can create shared experiences. They will remember the fun and excitement together. Plan a vacation. It doesn't have to be long, far away, or expensive. Get the children out of town together.

Sometimes a family memory will happen just because everyone is together. Create opportunities for these moments by including everyone in something you are doing. Encourage everyone to participate in a game or to watch a movie with you. Try to keep it short and light. Make it easy to participate. The idea is to have fun and involve everyone. If one or two decide not to join, go ahead without them. Often they will feel that they have missed out and be ready to join in later. You can play two different games with overlapping participants or rent a movie for the guys and one for the girls. We try to have family time on such a regular basis that one of our children created a blended family memory for us by naming these times "Forced Family Fun." They still join in.

Don't be discouraged if your planned opportunities don't create a special memory of one particular thing. Some of the best blended family memories come from a series of repeated events. Things like playing board games, football, or soccer in the backyard, or the family cuddled on the couch to watch a movie with popcorn. These are great memories too.

There is no need to plan something everyday. Sometimes, perhaps most of the time, you should leave the children alone together. Allow them to interact on their own terms. There will be disagreements. Don't worry; even natural siblings need a referee from time to time. If they are bored, you can suggest an activity or some "Forced Family Fun." But the more time they spend together, the greater the opportunity for blended family memories to be created. One of our memories came when a child with a new knock-knock joke book was tormenting her brothers and sisters. Finally she said "knock, knock" to one of her brothers who rendered her speechless (and created much relieved laughter) with his reply of "Come in!" It may not sound like much of a memory, but our children repeat it every time someone has a knock-knock joke.

Not all your family memories will include the whole family. Sometimes you just don't have everybody. If you have boys in both sets of children, let the boys (including the adult boy) go to a game or fishing together. Let all the girls enjoy an activity without the boys. If you are a first time parent of young girls, you can play dolls or have a tea party with them. Similarly, you can play ball or wrestle with your new boys. If you are doing something with your natural children, include your partner.

The holidays are, obviously, another great opportunity to create blended family memories. Invite all the children to participate in a family tradition. It can be a tradition that you or your partner has followed for a long time or you can create your own new tradition. Get everyone involved in baking goodies or decorating the house. It may be as simple as shooting fireworks on July 4th or reading the story about Jesus' birth on Christmas Eve. Since her children were babies, Dotti traced their hands, cut them out of red felt and hung all the hands on her Christmas tree. When we got married, she included my daughters in this tradition. Each year when we decorate the tree, we all get to see how much everyone has grown. Even the teenagers want to be sure their hands are on the tree. This tradition unites our children in yet another way.

Take pictures whenever you can. Some people are great at this. Dotti and I are not. We are usually so involved that we can only take a few pictures. It is not uncommon for one of our rolls of film to have pictures from a couple holidays and a birthday. We have found that you don't need many pictures. And we don't look at ours very often. But when one child does look, it seems as if the rest join in the remembering. And that is what we want.

Volunteer

When you volunteer to help with an activity that your child is involved in, your participation makes your child feel important. Volunteering for a stepchild shows that you also care for them. Volunteering also creates opportunities for blended family memories. Volunteer to be a coach or assistant coach of their favorite sport, find opportunities to volunteer at their school.

There are a myriad of places you can help outside the house. School, sports, church, scouts and others welcome volunteers. They usually will have a role that fits your available time. Whether it is bringing the after game snack once during a season or serving as room mother for a year.

Be careful that you do not take on too much. During the early part of creating your blended family, time will be at a premium. You will have more time to volunteer later in your blended family life. It may seem selfish, but you may wish to avoid volunteering for any activities that will be longer that one day during your first year of your blended family. After your first year, you will be better able to judge how much time you have available.

Your children appreciate your involvement. But you may have to explain that you can't be everyone's room mother or coach during the same year. If you have more than one child involved in the same activity or school, serving on a committee or board or just working at a special event is doubly appreciated. We once had four children at the same school. Dotti got to see and be seen by helping with the events at the school field day. Each of the children got some special attention from her that day.

Apologize

We all make mistakes. Whether we overreacted, forgot something, or put the wrong child on restriction, mistakes are a part of blending a family. As you begin to blend your family, your children will be watching to see how you handle your mistakes.

Your children probably know that you are not perfect. Recognizing your mistakes and apologizing for them builds respect for you among your children. It shows that you care about all of them and that you are fair.

The failure to apologize when you have erred can create problems in your home. You may be regarded as unfair or as showing favoritism. This, in turn, can create feelings of jealousy and mistrust.

When you make a mistake, admit it. A simple apology is usually enough. Sometimes your error will have caused a child to miss an event like going to the movies with a friend. Do what you can to rectify the situation. Perhaps you could take the child and a friend to the movies tomorrow.

The Rewards

Along with the trials of creating a blended family come some rewards. You get to be the parent of a new set of children, and that is a special privilege. There are times when you get to be a part of the growing up of your new children that their natural parent misses. You may get to enjoy the success of figuring out a difficult math problem or of the excitement of scoring well on a test that you helped your new child study hard for. You may get to watch as your new child goes door-to-door selling Girl Scout cookies. Those are things that are typically reserved for natural moms and dads.

Sometimes it can be hard to see this as a privilege because it can seem to be an extra burden. It's not. Once I skipped a meeting to watch my stepson help his team win a first round soccer tournament game. It went to overtime. He was the team's goalkeeper and had a couple important saves. In the next game, which was only an hour later, he gave up six second half goals. He was devastated. He was crying. As his mother and I crossed the field, he came running toward us. Dotti and I were surprised when he grabbed me. He and I went off alone to talk until he began to feel better. There are some things that a son can better share with a dad and a daughter with a mom. His natural father missed the games, but I had the privilege of being there for him. Because my heart ached for him, it didn't occur to me until later that we must have been doing something right.

Section Three
Relate with the Other Parents

One of the biggest challenges for blended families is that of relating with the other parents. We divorced our ex for a reason. It is likely, therefore, that there are some differences that still exist.

You may have settled into a reasonable routine for dealing with your other parent while you were a single parent. Your new relationship *will* affect your other parent. The effect may be unpredictable. The other parent may be more cooperative or they may become angry, jealous or suddenly territorial with your children.

Some people have a good relationship with their other parent. I hope this is true for your situation. Our relationship with our other parents has been more like a yo-yo. Sometimes it is civil and sometimes not. One of our other parents was upset when Dotti and I got married. It did not seem to bother the other.

Recognize that the fact you are beginning to blend a family can change your relationship with your other parent. That can be good or bad. Some other parents will do stupid things to sabotage your wedding. Some will deliberately try to make you angry. Some will simply try to take advantage of you. Some have been known to tell lies or make threats. Some will try to make you look bad in front of the children. Some will use the children in a continuing battle to get what they want. One friend believes that her new partner's other parent tried to sabotage her marriage. After our friend was married in May, the two teenagers who have never been allowed to spend more than a weekend with their father were left for the entire summer. This created an unanticipated strain because our friend had planned on having three full time children, not five. Under circumstances like these, we must find a way to relate to our other parents for the benefit of our children.

Communication with Other Parents

Whether you and your partner have a friendly relationship with all of your children's other parents or not, you must communicate day to day matters like schedule changes and daily living needs or concerns. Of course, you will always discuss any adjustments in visitation or holiday schedules and various financial issues as they arise.

You and your children's other parent have probably already decided what kinds of information need to be communicated. What information does your new partner share with their children's other parent? Perhaps the better question is at what point do you talk to the other parent. If a child is sick, do you tell the other parent at the first sign of a fever, if the child stays home from school or daycare or if a doctor's visit is required? It can be helpful to find out what your partner does with their other parent.

In some situations you may have called your other parent quickly before you began to blend a family because you needed their help. Now that you have a new partner, you probably won't call as quickly. If your other parent has been willing to help get your children to appointments or to watch a sick child, you can continue to allow them to help. You just don't have to rely upon them as much. Since you no longer have to rely upon them, the timing of some of your communication will change.

How do you actually communicate with the other parents? Obviously, you can talk in person or on the phone. If you find having a conversation with them difficult, call when you know that they won't be home and leave a message on their machine.

No machine, send a note or letter by mail. Be careful of sending notes or letters with the children—the note can get lost or forgotten and the child may feel stuck in the middle of your communication between the other parents. E-mail can provide distance in a conversation (and you can keep copies if it gets nasty). Emails, notes and messages on the answering machine allow the person receiving them to think about how they want to respond before they actually do. This may help in reducing potential conflict.

You can often share news about your child by encouraging your child to tell their other parent the news themselves. Our children can call with news about report cards, school programs and ball games or other extra-curricular activities. When one son broke his arm playing soccer, he called his dad after the x-rays. His mother filled in the details after they talked. When one of our daughters landed a part in a play, she called and we got the schedule information later. We don't send messages to our other parents through the children. We do encourage the children share news about themselves with their other parent. It is important communication but it also lets the children get the attention they deserve from their other parent and helps the other parent to feel more included in the children's lives.

Question the Other Parent

Even if you find it difficult to communicate with the other parent, there will be times when you cannot avoid it. There will be issues that need to be discussed. You may need to let your other parent know that you don't approve of one of their decisions regarding a child. You will need to question things that seem unusual. Remember, you cannot control what happens in the other household, so do not get caught up trying to control what you cannot control.

There is no easy way to do confront issues you may not agree on. Be bold and make the call. Discuss what you will say with your new partner before making the call to make sure you have a reasonable perspective. Give your new partner permission to disagree with you and give you an honest opinion. Once we were alarmed when we learned that the other parent had allowed a child to visit at a new friend's house because we knew that the friend's older sibling was confined to that house after being arrested on a drug charge. We did not believe that was a good place for our child to visit. Our other parents did not know about the problem with the friend's sibling and we were able to peacefully agree on a course of action. (The new friend could come visit at our house. Our child would not visit at the friend's house.) In other situations we have had to be satisfied with expressing our opinion without getting a satisfying resolution for us.

Don't forget that our children have learned to play one parent against another. The children are successful in this ploy only when you and the other parent do not communicate. Now that they have three or four parents, the children can get very creative. One of ours wanted to purchase a violent, mature rated video game. We had told him no. Our child reserved the game under the name of his mother when she was busy with another child. Later when he was at the store with his father, he tricked his father into believing that the game was acceptable because his mother had reserved it. His father let him buy it. Of course, when we talked with his (irate) dad later, his plan was discovered and the game went back to the store. This communication did not begin in the most pleasant way because his dad was upset with us because he believed we had approved an inappropriate game. But he did question an action of ours that seemed irregular and, once we talked, we were able to handle the situation together. When you communicate with the other parents, the children know and the whole family benefits. Working together as parents provide the children with a team of adults to help guide and monitor their lives in a healthy and successful way. The focus of parenting is on the children—not on which parent is always right or in control.

Share Calenders

Most of your communication with your other parent will be about plans and schedules. Good communication in this area will reduce conflicts and avoid stress for you and your children.

You and the other parent need to know what events the children have so that you can plan. Is there an event that your child wants both of their natural parents attend? If parental attendance is optional, you must know about the event in order to exercise your option. Do you need to send or get special clothes for the children for the weekend? Is there a family wedding to attend or a ski trip planned? As a blended-family parent you now get to do this for two sets of children.

Keep a calendar of household events and share it (or the pertinent parts) with the other parents. If your children are in school, make sure that you and the other parent have a copy of the school calendar. Share ball game and any other extra-curricular schedules. The earlier you can share this information, the easier it is for everyone to plan. Creating a family web page is another great way to share information. There are now several shared calendars available on the Internet. The calendar at www.familiez.com allows you to share the children's calendar without sharing your personal events. Having one central location that all family members can check every day will do wonders to reduce communication blunders and reduce potential for conflict.

A family web calendar could easily provide a way for all family members to enter in pertinent scheduling information. Some of the web calendars also provide email options or message boards that will allow for non-threatening communication between households. When you begin using such a method it will be important to check it daily for changes.

Support the Other Parent

Doing what is best for your children will occasionally require you to support your other parent. Your children need to respect and obey their other parent. You do not have to always agree with the other parent. Support their reasonable actions because you know that the other parent must maintain order in their household too.

You should support the other parent in the rules of their house. Their rules may be different from yours. You cannot set the rules for their house. And unless, you have evidence to the contrary, you must assume that they are doing what they believe is best for the children. Remember that the make up of their household may be different from yours therefore some of their rules and expectations will be different.

When you support the other parent in their decisions, you are only giving them a reasonable benefit of the doubt. You don't know all that has happened in their house. You do know that they are adults who usually act in the best interest of our children. You also know that our children (like all of us) will try to paint themselves in the best light in any given situation. If you decide to question the other parent, most of the time you find that they acted with cause.

Supporting the other parent doesn't always mean that you carry a discipline that is begun in their house into your house. It will mean that you tell your child that you agree with their other parent or that the child would be treated similarly if the same situation arose in your house. Or you may have to tell your child they need to obey their other parent even if they think the rules are unfair.

From time to time one of our other parents will do something that appears foolish or inconsistent. They will hurt the feelings of our child. They will make a promise to a child and break it. They will forget an event that is important to our child. When that happens, you must support the other parent. Remember that the relationship between your children and their other parent is important to them. They will have a relationship with their other parent for the rest of their lives. So, we find ourselves saying and doing things that encourage that relationship. Yes, this can mean saying nice things about their other parent and even helping the other parent when they make a mistake.

Your other parent may or may not always support you in your role as parent in your household. It is important that no matter if they do or do not always support you that you support them. Your children watch everything you do as a parent and even though they may not always be happy about your decisions they will recognize the parent that is fair, reasonable, caring and consistent and learn to trust and respect this parent. Part of the goal of all parents is to have a healthy and happy relationship with their children. Recognize that the word healthy comes before happy, however if the relationship is healthy chances greatly improve that the relationship will be happy.

Rely on Your Partner

One of the great things about blending a family is that you no longer have to handle your ex by yourself. Your new partner will want to help. A problem with your ex is not just your problem. It is a family problem. Your partner is a tremendous resource that is now available to you. You can rely on your partner to help you whenever you feel troubled by something your ex may have done.

If your partner has an ex too, he/she may have already faced a similar situation. At the very least your partner will have some different insights into the situation. Your partner can provide a sympathetic ear. Your partner can help you stay cool, when you are angry. They can often provide a perspective you have not thought of. If your partner is of the same gender as your ex your partner may be able to give you some insight into how your ex may view different situations as a man or woman. Sometimes just having another person by your side is a tremendous help.

When your ex is causing a problem, ask your partner for help. Let your partner help you plan a response if one is needed. Dotti has helped me create several effective responses to my ex. She has a different perspective than I do. She thinks like a woman and often can help to frame the response in a way that my ex will take it easier. Together we do better.

The Other Step Parent

When you began to blend your family, your children gained a stepparent. Your children may have another step-parent in their other house. They have to live with that other stepparent some of the time. Just as we want our children to have a good relationship with our partner, our children will benefit if they have a good relationship with the other stepparent.

How you interact with the other stepparent can be affected by jealousies, lack of trust, and anything your ex may have said about you. The other stepparent is often going to publicly support their partner in any disagreement with you. These things can make it difficult for us to encourage our children to have a relationship with the other stepparent.

Our children can benefit from having another caring adult in their lives. My teenage daughters have come to their stepmother, Dotti, for advice on matters that most teenagers would not talk to their mothers about. Where and what kind of advice would they get if they could not talk to Dotti? One of our teenage sons relies upon his stepmother to intercede with his dad, where we cannot. Encourage your children to develop their own relationship with the other stepparent. Your children do not necessarily have to love either stepparent, but they do have to respect them as adults and it is easier to get along if the children can develop some kind of healthy relationship with stepparents.

If you can learn to trust that the other stepparent has the best interests of your children in mind, you may even be able to find an occasional ally. The other stepparent may be a little more willing to listen and to help you find a solution to any difficulties between you and your ex. The other stepparent doesn't have all the emotional baggage that your ex does with you. They may have their own children and understand your concerns. Finding a solution helps both households. You know how difficult your ex can be. Appeal to the good sense of the other stepparent and give them a chance to help.

Handling Conflict

You will have conflicts with one or both parents. You will disagree on some issues. You may even be in court over support or custody issues. Through these conflicts you must continue to communicate. And you must be concerned about the effect your disagreement has upon your children.

Open conflict with the other parent creates confusion and stress for our children. The children don't know whom to believe as they have the potential to feel put in the middle. The children don't want to disobey or disappoint either of their parents. They may not fully understand the problem. They may feel guilty because they may believe that they caused the problem in some way. Think about it—my parents are fighting over or about me—therefore I must be the problem. If they did not have me maybe they would not fight so much. I love both my parents and feel that I am a part of them so when either parent puts the other down in front of me I also feel put down.

Avoid discussing these issues and arguing in front of the children. Do not begin and refuse to participate in any discussion of the issues that are in conflict in the hearing of the children. If lawyers are involved, you can use your lawyer as a reason not to talk about the issue. If you are talking with the other parent on the phone, go to your bedroom or some other private room and shut the door. Shortly after we were married, we were embroiled in a court battle with one of our other parents. The other parents were eager to discuss the issue at every opportunity, which inevitably led to a disagreement and made us all angry. Worse it upset the children. We wasted hours calming children and ourselves over the course of the year that it took to resolve the matter. We suffered a lot of needless heartache for an order that made a couple of changes that we agreed on before it started. You can avoid most of this mess by not getting out of the car when picking up your children. Call ahead for the children and tell them you are on the way or close so that they can be ready. Use notes, letters and answering machine messages as much as possible. Discussing court issues out of court will not help resolve the issue and can even make it worse. Think about it, if you could have resolved the issue outside of court you would not be going to court in the first place.

When you have an out of court conflict with the other parent, discuss and decide with your partner what you think the best solution for the children is. Tell the other parent and give them your reasons for your solution. You can try to resolve these conflicts over the phone, by notes, letters, or e-mail. We once tried to sit down at a restaurant over a cup of coffee. That may work for you. All it did for us was to keep the noise down. You may need to have several conversations over a period of time to sort some of these issues out. Recognize that you and your ex probably didn't communicate very well when you were together. It often can be more difficult now.

On some issues you may be in a position that allows you to decide and impose your will upon the other parent. Listen to their concerns anyway. You may find the roles reversed in the future and want the same courtesy. If the decision is completely in the hands of the other parent, give them your opinions about what you think is best and be willing to agree to disagree. Do not let their decision become an open ongoing battle. Remember you cannot make them do anything they do not want to do.

Do not waste your time and energy fighting things you cannot change. Find a way to let your children win. My wife and I have backgrounds in medicine and law that lead us to believe that a riding a motorcycle is dangerous. Dotti's ex purchased a motorcycle. Although we shared our concerns with the other parent, we cannot prevent him from riding the children on his motorcycle. We did make sure that the children have helmets and understand that they are to wear the helmets every time they are on the motorcycle. We educated the children to the dangers of head injuries and explained why it is important to wear helmets when they ride any type of two-wheeled vehicle. We let the children win by ensuring their safety and by not making a major issue over something we cannot control.

Different Parenting Styles

As we said earlier, children seem to adjust to different sets of rules in different households. How do we handle different styles of parenting with our children's other parents? Your other parent may be stricter than you are. You may practice your faith more vigorously than they do. There will be differences in each household that your children will have to learn to adjust to.

The other parent's style is often reflected in the children when they come to you. Your children may try to bring the rules they like into your house (Daddy lets me do it!) Or they may push your rules to the limit in reaction to returning from a household with different rules.

The best way to handle different styles of parenting is to accept that there are differences between you and the other parent. You have no control over the ordinary events at your children's other house. You cannot set their bedtime or control how much TV they watch or even what they watch. You aren't going to allow your other parent to set the rules for your house either. If you have a continuing problem, tell the other parent about it and give your reasons. You cannot make them change these style issues so do not continue to try to control things you cannot control. This will only frustrate you and make you upset. When your children point out the differences in an attempt to get you to change your rule simply explain to them that things are different in each house sometimes and that you know they will adjust to the differences.

In special situations, you may ask for help. When one of our children has a soccer game and is staying at his other parents house the night before, we ask that the child be put to bed at a reasonable hour. We have even suggested a time. Sometimes the other parent gets the child to bed and sometimes not (in fairness, sometimes the child has disobeyed). Usually your requests for simple things like this when backed up by solid reasons that benefit the child will be considered and get results. It just won't work every time. Do not get over focused on the times it does not work. Recognize and express your appreciation when your ex follows through with a suggestion. Avoid criticizing when they do not as criticism often leads to rebellion or resistance.

In the same way, you must do what it best for your household considering all the children. How do you send a child to bed early for an event you didn't know about when you promised that they could have a friend spend the night? You may be able to find a compromise. Whatever your style, listen to requests that the other parent has and let them know that they have been heard, and then do what you think is best for your children at your house.

Failure to supervise your children or questions regarding whether or not your children are receiving proper care are not differences in style. These issues will need to be addressed quickly and formally.

Visitation

When the time comes for the children to change houses, you will regularly interact with the other parent. If you live nearby, the changes will occur frequently. These can be times of high stress for you, your ex and your children.

The stress level can change once you begin to blend a family. Some other parents will be more accepting of a new partner than others. Very quickly one of our other parents didn't seem to care which of us came to pick-up or deliver the children. But, for many years the other was offended if the natural parent didn't come and let it be known.

You can ease some of the stress by establishing a routine or continuing the routine you already have. Over time bring your partner into the visitation mix by taking them along. Include your partner whether it is for a time of visitation or a special event. You will want to include your partner because there will be times that your schedule will require that your partner get your children without you. Building a sense of trust that your partner can handle the task is more easily accomplished if you start out adding them to the mix rather than just letting them do it on their own too soon.

Another way to relieve some of the stress is to communicate with the other parent about your schedule. If there is a change, let the other parent know as soon as possible. Call ahead to let the children know you'll be there soon so that they can get ready. If the other parent makes you angry every time you change children, avoid talking to them by staying in the car or your home. If your children are too young for this tactic, try having your partner or a friend with you for support. This can also work if the other parent wants to tell you all about their personal life and you don't really care to hear it. Having another person as support can be a reasonable excuse for why you cannot stay and listen to a lot of details.

Timeliness

Each of our divorce decrees has set times for visitation. Some other parents will be very strict with these time limits and others seem to view them as general guidelines. How we handle our other parents' timeliness can ease or create stress for our children and ourselves.

You know your other parents views about timeliness. Plan accordingly. If your other parent is strict with you about times, communicate with them if you are running late. A phone call is usually sufficient if you are a few minutes late. If you regularly run a few minutes late, get your partner to help you watch the time. Set an alarm clock or ask your children to help. We found we were running late because we were gathering everything together at the last minute. We always had trouble finding something. Now we get it all together after lunch (or most of it) and find it easier to leave on time. (A side benefit to this has been fewer forgotten items, like schoolbooks and toys.) A little planning helps avoid unnecessary stress for all.

Maybe your other parent is the one who is consistently late. You couldn't change them when you lived with them and you probably can't now. Your anger only hurts you and your children. If your other parent is prompt to get the children but late on the return, try doing the same to them. You or one of the children can call ahead of time as a reminder or just to help gauge the time of the other parent's arrival. If they are bringing the children to you allow for their tardiness by leaving some extra time between the children's scheduled arrival and the start of any event. Perhaps you have the children and have plans that are scheduled to begin at or near the pick up time. Make arrangements for the children to be watched or to stay with a friend or neighbor for a few minutes. Your other parent may not care if your plans are interrupted. You and your children benefit when you plan ahead.

If your other parent is consistently late, you can take advantage of the extra time with your children or with your partner. When our children were with us on different weekends, we often had thirty minutes to an hour of couple time when the other parent was late returning the children. Take that time to share a cup of coffee or a walk around the yard. If you have some extra time with the children, do something you enjoy that can be interrupted or is of short duration. Throw or kick a ball. Begin watching a movie on a tape that the children can take with them. Play a game with the agreement that whoever is ahead when the other parent arrives is the winner. Be prepared for the other parent's late arrival. You are in charge of your reactions and you can choose to be miserable, frustrated and angry or you can choose to turn the situation into something positive and happy.

Reciprocation

As long as the other parent is not putting your children in danger, the behavior of the other parent should not affect the basis for your decisions. The behavior of the other parent may affect how you make decisions and the decisions you make. Continue to make your decisions based on what is best for your children.

Do not expect the other parent to reciprocate your kindness or to put the children first in their lives. Some will, some won't. It doesn't matter if the other parent is as flexible and unselfish as you are. The other parent may even take advantage of your flexibility and unselfishness. This is not a contest; it doesn't have to be fair.

The other parent will do things that anger and frustrate you. The other parent may do something that requires you to cancel your long-standing plans. They may ruin a dinner or an entire weekend. Don't let your anger (however justified) prevent you from doing what is best for your children. Share your anger and frustration with your partner. Share it with the other parent. Then, make it easy for your children. Focus on taking care of them and on what you can do to make the situation better when they are with you.

Constantly remind yourself that you are only in control of what you do and that trying to change other people does not work. Putting external pressure on others to change often backfires. If you really want other people to change then change the way you interact with them. Be positive, listen, support, encourage, and respect them. Show them respect and you will eventually get respect back. Trust that they will do what is best for the children even if they do it differently than you do. Barring neglect or abuse, understand that their way is different than yours.

Events for Everyone

Every child will be involved in events that are open to the public. There are school programs and concerts, games and events at church or scouts. These are special times for our children. We are going to be there. The child's other parent will often be there too.

How we interact with the other parent at these events can affect our children. We can ruin our child's event or embarrass them. The interaction between ourselves and the other parents can be a non-issue as long as we work to make it such.

If you and the other parent have a genial relationship, these events should cause few problems. Be sure that your children get the congratulations and attention that both parents have to offer. Often this is no more than asking your child to go find their other parent or of you going to find your child. If your relationship with the other parent is not very good, you can pre-arrange a place to meet your child after the event. Meet or have them meet their other parent at the concession stand or by the front door. Have your child tell the other parent of these plans before the event, if possible. If you are providing transportation, allow your child time to get the praise and attention they deserve from their other parent without rushing them if possible.

Events like High School graduations and weddings can require a lot more planning. These are major events for your child and they will be old enough to help plan and co-ordinate. When our oldest graduated from High School, our plans had to take into consideration the tensions that still exist between her natural parents. We arranged for one parent to take all of their pictures first. We planned so that the drop-in we held for family and friends did not conflict with the party her mother hosted. Even if you and the other parent get along well, planning and comparing schedules will reduce the chance of any conflict.

There are some events like weddings where you will have to take turns and share. The more decisions you can make before the event, the less chance of frictions during the event. There are money decisions like who is paying for the wedding, the reception or the rehearsal dinner. There are timing decisions regarding who goes first. You must decide seating arrangements. Seek the help of a wedding planner or someone who has recently had a wedding to make sure you haven't overlooked any areas of potential conflict. Early decision-making on some of these issues makes it easier to be fair to everybody. Don't forget that those who take the last turn often have a little more time.

Major events are emotional and stressful. When we are emotional and under stress, we are more easily provoked into conflict. Even good relationships can become strained. Remember that this is your child's event. Many times you will just have to grin and bear it for your child's sake.

Conclusion

Your relationship with your other parent will change when you begin to blend a family. As with every other aspect of blending your family, relating with the other parents is more difficult at the beginning. Over time you will develop a routine for them and your interactions will become more peaceful. It is up to you to manage your behavior and to maintain a positive interaction with all involved, no matter how they respond or treat you.

Final Thoughts

These are just a few ideas to help you create your blended family. These ideas have worked for others and us. These have been learned on the job as we blended our own family.

This book is based upon my experience. There are some things that I have not experienced. Yet if you apply the general principals here, you can create a wonderful blended family. Love your partner. Put your children needs first immediately after your partners. Don't let the other parent prevent you from doing either of the first two.

Blending your family will require love, hope and strength. You have these already. You love or you couldn't have begun your relationship with your new partner. You have hope because you can see a future with your new partner in a blended family. And you have strength because the old adage that two are stronger than one is true. There are other attributes that you will need, but these three will see you through.

Approach everyone in your blended family with a willingness to listen, encourage, support, trust and respect. Do this and people will learn to eventually return your efforts in kind.

One last bit of practical advice. Go find your partner right now or grab them when they get home. Tell them you love them and give them a kiss. Share with them an idea from this book you would like to try.

Printed in the United States
71370LV00002B/25